21st
Century
Skills Library

COOL CAREERS

CHEF

JOSH GREGORY

WITHDRAWN

Published in the United States of America by
Cherry Lake Publishing, Ann Arbor, Michigan
www.cherrylakepublishing.com

Content Adviser
Jacob Larson, Associate of Culinary Science

Credits
Photos: Cover and page 1, ©iStockphoto.com/kemalbas; pages 4 and 23,
©iStockphoto.com/Juanmonino; page 6, ©iStockphoto.com/Wellmony; pages 9
and 28, ©iStockphoto.com/kcline; page 10, ©Siarhei Fedarenka/Shutterstock,
Inc.; page 12, ©visi.stock/Shutterstock, Inc.; page 15 and 21, ©Monkey Business
Images/Shutterstock, Inc.; page 16, ©iStockphoto.com/1001nights; page 18,
©iStockphoto.com/Thomas_EyeDesign; page 24, ©iStockphoto.com/RadeLukovic;
page 27, ©OtnaYdur/Shutterstock, Inc.

Library of Congress Cataloging-in-Publication Data
Gregory, Josh.
   Chef/by Josh Gregory.
      p. cm.—(Cool careers)
   Includes bibliographical references and index.
   ISBN-13: 978-1-60279-985-1 (lib. bdg.)
   ISBN-10: 1-60279-985-7 (lib. bdg.)
   1. Cooks—Vocational guidance—Juvenile literature. 2. Cooking—Juvenile literature.
I. Title. II. Series.
   TX652.5.G725 2011
   641.5092—dc22   2010029085

Cherry Lake Publishing would like to acknowledge
the work of The Partnership for 21st Century Skills.
Please visit *www.21stcenturyskills.org* for more information.

Printed in the United States of America
Corporate Graphics Inc.
January 2011
CLSP08

COOL CAREERS

TABLE OF CONTENTS

CHAPTER ONE
MORE THAN JUST COOKING

Elizabeth studied the **menu** in front of her. "I don't know what to order," she said. "There are too many good choices."

Chefs work hard to make sure your meal comes out just the way you like it.

It was Elizabeth's birthday. Her parents had taken her to her favorite Italian restaurant to celebrate. Elizabeth set her menu aside for a moment. She took a bite of the crusty garlic bread the waiter had brought out. "Mmm, delicious!" she said.

She picked up the menu again and decided what to order.

"What would you like tonight?" asked the waiter.

"I'll have the pasta Alfredo with chicken," said Elizabeth. "Can I also have a salad?"

"Of course," replied the waiter. He collected the menus after her parents ordered. "I'll be back soon with your dinner."

He hurried to the kitchen with the order for Elizabeth's family. The chef and her kitchen staff made sure Elizabeth's birthday dinner was prepared perfectly.

■ ■ ■

No matter what kind of restaurant you visit, there are people working hard in the kitchen to prepare tasty food. The chef is in charge of all of these workers. He works hard to make sure everything goes smoothly.

A chef is responsible for coming up with the recipes that are on the menu. He uses his taste and knowledge of food to decide which ingredients go best together. He might even spend his free time testing new ideas. Many restaurants change their menus often. Some change their menus along with the seasons. Other restaurants might change their menus every week. These restaurants often have only a few choices on the menu at a time.

It is a chef's job to make sure the menu makes sense. He must think carefully about the style of food served at his restaurant. Picture a restaurant that specializes in healthy food. Would the owners be happy to find greasy cheeseburgers on the menu? The appetizers and side dishes should **complement** the main courses. There should be a variety of tastes and **textures**. A very spicy side dish is

Every meal needs the right balance of textures and flavors.

not the best match for a very spicy main course. The chef also needs to decide how big each serving should be for all items on the menu. For chefs at fancier restaurants, creating the menu can be the biggest challenge of all. They use ingredients and cooking methods that many people might not be used to.

21ST CENTURY CONTENT

Years ago, some ingredients could only be easily found in certain parts of the world. Many people did not know about the recipes enjoyed by people of other **cultures**. Now you can find almost any kind of food if you look hard enough. Chefs can order ingredients from around the world. Sometimes, they travel to faraway cities and countries. They learn about different flavors and bring their ideas to other chefs. This means we have a wider variety of foods to choose from when we go out to eat.

Chefs choose ingredients carefully. They need to make sure the food they prepare is fresh and tasty. They must make sure the ingredients are not too expensive. For example, a chef might want to use a rare spice in his new seafood dish.

If he uses the spice, however, the dish will be very expensive. He doesn't think enough customers will be willing to pay the high price. He decides to think of a less-expensive spice that will work well enough.

It is often the chef's job to purchase ingredients from suppliers. After planning the menu and deciding which ingredients will be needed, he places an order. Supply companies deliver the ingredients to the restaurant in big trucks. Meat, produce, and spices might all come from different companies.

The chef keeps track of which items are needed at which times. He might only need to order items such as dried spices once in a while. The restaurant can store large amounts of these things because they do not spoil easily. Meat might be delivered every day so that it is always fresh. The amount of ingredients needed depends on the size of the restaurant and how many customers it serves each day.

Chefs also need to keep their kitchens clean. They must follow any **health codes** that are set by local governments. Restaurants that do not follow these codes can be fined or shut down. Chefs must also make sure that food is cooked properly. People will not go back to restaurants that made them sick!

If chefs pay careful attention to all of this, they will likely be rewarded with many customers. Sometimes, chefs become so popular that people come from around the world to eat their food!

Some chefs visit markets to find the very best fruits and vegetables.

CHAPTER TWO
IN THE KITCHEN

C hefs usually spend much of their time in kitchens. Chefs must master a wide variety of cooking skills and methods. They trim meat to prepare it for cooking. They quickly chop vegetables and herbs.

Chefs use a variety of knives to prepare different dishes.

Chefs must know how to create different kinds of sauces, doughs, and **marinades**. These can be just as important as meat and vegetables. What would a pizza be, for example, without a delicious crust?

Chefs use many tools to transform ingredients into meals. Knives come in different sizes. There are many kinds of blades. Each type is designed for cutting certain foods. A short, stiff blade works well for removing bones from meat. A knife with a **serrated** edge can cut through soft foods such as bread without crushing them. Knowing which knife works best in each situation is an important skill for any cook.

Knives aren't the only tools chefs use to cut ingredients. Grinders can turn meat into hamburger or sausage. Spice grinders can crush hard items such as peppercorns into powder for seasoning. Blenders and food processors can quickly turn ingredients into liquids for use in sauces or soups.

It is also important for a chef to know which pots and pans are best for cooking different foods. It wouldn't be very practical to cook soup in a frying pan. A chef must choose the right type of cookware based on its shape and size. A chef must also understand the materials each piece of cookware is made of. Aluminum and copper heat up quickly, but they do not hold heat well. This makes them good for cooking food that needs to get hot quickly, but not very good for slow cooking. Some cookware is better for cooking in an oven. Other kinds are better choices for cooking on a stove top.

Knowing how to apply heat to food is often one of the most important and difficult cooking skills. After all, most people do not like to eat food that is burned or undercooked. Learning to tell when food is done cooking or needs to be turned over can take a lot of practice. Chefs learn how to cook using ovens, grills, stove tops, and other heating tools. Some recipes even call for the use of a small torch.

It takes a lot of practice to be able to heat food to just the right temperature.

Most chefs specialize in a certain kind of **cuisine**. Sometimes, they stick to the traditions of a **regional** or **ethnic** cuisine. These chefs learn all they can about a certain cooking style. They prepare meals that have been popular for a long time. Some chefs make small changes to the traditional recipes. This helps them stand out from other chefs who cook in the same style.

LEARNING & INNOVATION SKILLS

Jacob Larson has cooked in food establishments of all kinds, from small sandwich shops to full-service restaurants. His experiences have taught him many lessons. For one thing, it is important for everyone in the kitchen to work hard and as a team. This means being willing to help one another. As Jacob puts it, "No matter how high you climb up the ladder, you will still do dishes from time to time."

Even though it is a lot of work, Jacob loves his job. "Nothing beats having the opportunity to eat and learn how to make delicious food while getting paid!"

A chef can't do all of a restaurant's cooking alone. At some restaurants, the chef might not do much cooking at all. Most of the cooking may be handled by the other cooks in the kitchen. Most chefs start out as one of these cooks and work their way up to higher positions.

A **sous chef** is second-in-command to the head chef. He or she supervises the rest of the kitchen staff when the chef is busy with other responsibilities.

Some restaurants have line cooks. Each line cook has a station where he does a certain job. Each station has the tools and ingredients the line cook needs. This helps the cooks quickly prepare many meals at once.

Small restaurants with simple menus might have short-order cooks. These cooks are usually found at diners or sandwich shops. They can quickly prepare simple meals such as hamburgers or fried eggs.

Food preparation workers help the other cooks by doing simple jobs. These include chopping vegetables and measuring ingredients. They might also help make sure the kitchen is free of clutter. These jobs help save time for the other cooks.

Not all chefs work in restaurants. Some of them work in kitchens at hotels, schools, and hospitals. Others work as **caterers** or personal chefs. Caterers cook for parties or events. They know how to cook a lot of food at once. Personal chefs work in the home kitchens of the people who hire them. They plan menus, shop for groceries, and prepare meals in a person's home.

Chefs handle many different jobs. No matter what chefs do, though, they must know a lot about food and cooking.

The sous chef checks in with the rest of the kitchen staff to make sure everything is going smoothly.

CHAPTER THREE
BECOMING A CHEF

Becoming a chef takes a lot of hard work. Chefs need to learn a variety of special skills. This can take

Culinary arts students learn all of the basic skills they will need to work in a restaurant kitchen.

years of practice. Many chefs start their careers by getting an education in the culinary arts. The culinary arts relate to the skillful preparation of food.

Many community colleges and technical schools offer culinary arts programs. There are also special culinary arts schools. Some future chefs choose to enroll in hospitality programs. An education in hospitality does not just cover cooking. It also involves the skills a chef might need to open and run her own restaurant. Most culinary arts or hospitality programs take 2 years to complete. Some hospitality programs can take as long as 4 years, though.

Culinary arts students take classes to help them learn basic cooking skills. They learn about knife skills and different ways to cook food. They learn how to use and care for kitchen equipment. Nutrition classes help them learn how to create food that is both healthy and tasty. Classes in menu planning and portion control help prepare them for the duties of a head chef. Other classes teach students how to use ingredients in ways that limit waste. They also learn how to store food so it won't spoil.

Internships and **apprenticeships** are another important part of a chef's education. These allow chefs to get on-the-job experience at real restaurants. It is important for chefs to get as much experience as possible. Few restaurants will hire chefs or cooks who have never worked in kitchens. Some large restaurants and hotels offer special training programs of their own.

After graduating from culinary arts programs and working as apprentices, chefs need to work their way up through the ranks. Beginning chefs usually work as line cooks or food preparation workers. Some might start out as servers. In order to move up, they need to show that they can work hard. They must prove that they have the skills needed to keep a kitchen running smoothly. It can take many years to advance from a beginning cook to a head chef.

Beginning chefs often start out doing simple jobs like cutting vegetables.

LIFE & CAREER SKILLS

There are many options for people who are serious about becoming professional chefs. The American Culinary Federation (ACF) is the largest organization of professional chefs in North America. The ACF offers services to help future chefs. More than 200 culinary arts programs in North America are accredited by the ACF. If something is accredited, it is recognized as having met certain standards. The organization also helps place students in apprenticeships. Chefs can get certifications from the ACF, too. Being certified shows you have reached a certain standard or passed a test. Restaurants are more likely to hire chefs with certifications.

Chefs and cooks need strong senses of taste and smell. These help them figure out which ingredients a recipe needs more or less of. They also help chefs avoid serving food that tastes bad!

Chefs also need to be able to think creatively. This helps them come up with recipes that other chefs haven't thought of.

A kitchen can be a stressful place to work. Things move very quickly. It can be hot, crowded, and loud. Chefs and cooks need to be able to handle the pressure. They must stay calm even if the restaurant is very busy or something goes wrong.

Chefs often work long hours. They are tired by the end of the workday. But chefs must always stay alert. The kitchen can be a dangerous place for anyone who isn't paying attention. Knives and stoves are important tools, but they can cause cuts and burns.

Chefs need to be able to do many things at once. Sometimes a restaurant has many customers who all want different meals to eat. When this happens, chefs and cooks might need to keep an eye on one dish in the oven while chopping ingredients for a different dish. Being able to pay attention to many things at the same time is crucial. If a chef can't do this, he might make mistakes. Imagine if a chef forgot about something in the oven. Or if he cut himself because he got distracted. Chefs need to be as **efficient** as possible. There is never any time to waste in a busy kitchen.

Kitchen workers need to be able to work well in groups. Food preparation workers and line cooks need to do their jobs quickly so the other cooks aren't delayed. Chefs, sous chefs, and other leaders in the kitchen must pay attention to what everyone is doing. They need to assign jobs to the right

It can be very stressful to make sure that each meal turns out perfectly.

people and make sure no steps are forgotten. Everyone must communicate and work together to keep delicious meals flowing out of the kitchen.

Chefs who open their own restaurants or work as caterers must learn about accounting, management, and other business skills. They need to know how to advertise their businesses and deal with customers. In some ways, running your own business can be more difficult than working for someone else.

 LIFE & CAREER SKILLS

Some chefs choose to open their own restaurants. This gives them more freedom in creating menus. It also means a lot of extra work. Chefs who own restaurants will often hire managers to help with these extra duties. Managers might be in charge of hiring and firing servers or hosts. They make sure repairs are made when something in the restaurant breaks down. Sometimes they help the chef order food. Many restaurant managers get their degrees in hospitality or food service management.

Restaurant owners often have to put in long hours for their businesses to be successful.

CHAPTER FOUR
COOKING INTO THE FUTURE

J obs for chefs are expected to increase in the next few years. The best chefs will compete for jobs at top

Skilled chefs with ideas for flavorful new dishes are welcome restaurant team members.

restaurants. Only the most popular and creative chefs will find work at these kinds of places.

How much chefs make depends on where they work and what they do. Most chefs and head cooks make between $29,000 and $51,000 per year. The lowest-paid chefs made less than $22,000. The highest-paid chefs made more than $66,000.

21ST CENTURY CONTENT

Why is there so much competition for chef jobs at nice restaurants? One reason is financial—those jobs tend to pay more. Other cooks usually make less money. In 2008, for example, most restaurant cooks made between $18,230 and $26,150. Short-order cooks made between $16,280 and $23,450. Fast-food cooks made between $15,470 and $19,240. Many of these cooks need to have more than one job to earn the money they need.

Jobs will be created as more new restaurants open. Today's restaurant customers want more dining choices. They want restaurants that are closer to their homes and ones that produce quality meals quickly. There's a good chance that restaurants and chefs that meet these expectations will have success in the future.

Chefs are an important part of our culture. They help shape our tastes and diets. Becoming a successful chef takes a lot of hard work and commitment. But the rewards can be great. Do you have what it takes to make it in this industry?

21ST CENTURY CONTENT

Many people lead busy lives. They don't always have time to cook dinner, but they don't want to eat unhealthy fast food. There are now many television shows that teach people how to cook fast, easy meals. There are also restaurants that specialize in fast, healthy takeout meals. Do you have any ideas for healthy food that can be prepared quickly? If so, you might be on your way to becoming a popular chef!

What tasty foods will chefs come up with next?

Will you become a chef someday?

SOME WELL-KNOWN CHEFS

Rick Bayless (1953–) is a chef and owner of the Frontera Grill and Topolobampo restaurants in Chicago. He specializes in Mexican cooking. Topolobampo is one of the only fine-dining Mexican restaurants in the United States. Bayless has also written several cookbooks and has a PBS TV show called *Mexico: One Plate at a Time*.

Anthony Bourdain (1956–) is a chef and author of several books about restaurants and cooking. His book *Kitchen Confidential*, about what it is like to work in a restaurant kitchen, was a best seller. He is the host of the TV show *Anthony Bourdain: No Reservations*. The show follows him as he travels the world eating interesting foods and meeting new people.

Alton Brown (1962–) is the host of *Good Eats* on the Food Network. The show teaches people to cook while showing the science and history behind the recipes. He got the idea for *Good Eats* while working as a video director. He liked watching cooking shows between shoots. He decided that cooking shows could be more exciting, so he quit his job and entered culinary school. He has also written several cookbooks and starred in other TV cooking shows.

Julia Child (1912–2004) helped popularize French cooking in the United States. She studied cooking in Paris after moving to France with her husband. The cookbook she wrote with two friends, *Mastering the Art of French Cooking*, was a huge success. She was also the host of several TV cooking shows.

Emeril Lagasse (1959–) is best known as the host of several TV cooking shows. These include *Emeril Live* and *Essence of Emeril*. Fans enjoy his energetic style of cooking. He also owns several restaurants and has written many best-selling cookbooks.

GLOSSARY

apprenticeships (uh-PREN-tiss-shipss) periods of time during which people learn a trade by working with skilled and experienced professionals

caterers (KAY-tur-urz) people who provide food for parties or other events

complement (KOM-pluh-muhnt) to go well with

cuisine (kwi-ZEEN) a style or way of cooking or presenting food

cultures (KUHL-churz) the ways of life of different groups of people

efficient (uh-FISH-uhnt) able to work well without wasting energy or time

ethnic (ETH-nik) having to do with a group of people who have the same culture or history

health codes (HELTH KOHDZ) rules set up by a local government for how a kitchen must be kept clean and organized in order to prevent sickness

internships (IN-turn-shipss) periods of employment often taken on by students to gain experience

marinades (mair-uh-NAYDZ) flavorful liquids in which foods are soaked before cooking

menu (MEN-yoo) a list of foods served at a restaurant

regional (REE-juh-nuhl) having to do with a certain area

serrated (SER-ay-tid) having notches or teeth like a saw

sous chef (SOO SHEF) the second-in-command to a head chef in a kitchen

textures (TEKS-churz) the feel or look of things

FOR MORE INFORMATION

BOOKS

Dunn, Mary R. *I Want to Be a Chef.* New York: PowerKids Press, 2009.

Klein, Hilary Dole. *A Day with a Chef.* Mankato, MN: The Child's World, 2008.

Thompson, Lisa. *Creating Cuisine: Have You Got What It Takes to Be a Chef?* Minneapolis: Compass Point Books, 2008.

WEB SITES

American Culinary Federation
www.acfchefs.org
Visit the official Web site of the American Culinary Federation to learn more about apprenticeships and culinary education.

Bureau of Labor Statistics—Chefs, Head Cooks, and Food Preparation and Serving Supervisors
www.bls.gov/oco/ocos330.htm
Learn more about what it takes to become a chef and what chefs do.

KidsHealth—Recipes
kidshealth.org/kid/recipes/index.html
Try your hand at being a chef with these recipes. Be sure to have an adult help.

INDEX

ABOUT THE AUTHOR

Josh Gregory is an author and editor. He lives in Chicago, Illinois. Though he is not a chef, he does manage to cook plenty of delicious meals at home.